VOICES THROUGH SKIN

POEMS

THERESA
SENATO
EDWARDS

SiblingRivalryPress

Sibling Rivalry Press, LLC
13913 Magnolia Glen Drive
Alexander, AR 72002

www.siblingrivalrypress.com

Library of Congress Control Number: 2011921938

ISBN: 978-0-9832931-0-1

First Sibling Rivalry Press Edition, June 2011

ACKNOWLEDGEMENTS

Grateful acknowledgement is made to the editors of the following literary journals and anthologies in which the following poems or earlier versions of them first appeared and/or were reprinted:

AdmitTwo: "Painting Czeslawa Kwoka" in collaboration with Lori Schreiner's paintings of Czeslawa based on Wilhelm Brasse photographs

Atticus Books: republish of "Lady"

Autumn Sky Poetry: "Clinic" and republish of "Painting Czeslawa Kwoka"

Blackmail Press: "Riot in the Local High School, 1975," "River. Snow.," "Walls," and "Your Attempt"

Blue Earth Review: "Her Rituals" and "Lady"

Boxcar Poetry Review: "Back Seat. 1965   Forward, Back"

Chronogram: "Battered" and "Bending"

The Circle (Marist College newspaper): "Caitlin"

Clean Sheets Magazine: "D.J.E." and "With Guilt"

decomP magazine: "The Game Show Hour."

Flutter Poetry Journal: "Inventing Dead"

The Orange Room Review: "Hot Tea Cooled"

Pirene's Fountain: "After Surgery"

Pitkin Review: "Because You're Alive" and "Mother's Day"

Press 1: "Closet" and "On Your Back"

Seven CirclePress: "Flat & Hollow" and "Healing"

SNReview: "The Nurse on Percy," "The Smell of Alcohol," and "What Was Left"

SOFTBLOW: "Joanie Bach" and "She Didn't Eat Her"

Touch: The Journal of Healing: "The Touch of the Notch"

Triplopia: "Rats," "The Smell of Cigarette Smoke," and a republish of "The Nurse on Percy"

"Flat & Hollow" and "Healing" were included in *Seven CirclePress'* first print anthology *CircleShow Vol. 1*.

"Back Seat. 1965   Forward, Back" was included in *Boxcar Poetry Review's* second print anthology.

"Painting Czeslawa Kwoka" was read during *Poetry Super Highway's* Open Poetry Reading, BlogTalkRadio, February 2009.

"Painting Czeslawa Kwoka" is included in a collaborative book with Lori Schreiner entitled *Painting Czeslawa Kwoka ~ Honoring Children of the Holocaust*.

"Painting Czeslawa Kwoka" collaboration was included in *Holly Rose Review*, February 2009, special addition to the PEACE Issue for Facebook, limited viewing.

"Painting Czeslawa Kwoka" collaboration was shown at the Windham Art Gallery, part of *Words and Images: A collaborative show of artists and writers*, June 2007, Brattleboro, VT; Exner Block Gallery, part of *Words and Images*: second showing, July 2007, Bellows Falls, Vermont.

"Painting Czeslawa Kwoka" collaboration was awarded The Tacenda Literary Award for Best Collaboration, 2007, from BleakHouse Publishing.

Thank you to my family: Richard and Carmen Senato, Doug and Troy Edwards.

A special thank you goes to Bea Gates and Jane Wohl for their guidance.

A special remembrance goes to Alice Siegel and Ruth Schonthal, who both heard my voice many years ago in my music.

And I thank God because when I am alone with my inspiration, I believe I am never quite alone.

for my family ~ Doug, Troy, Richard and Carmen
and in loving memory of my parents ~ Tessie and Tony Senato

Even during war, moments of delicate peace
Arrive; ceaseless the water ripples, love
Speaks through the river in its human voices.

~ Muriel Rukeyser, "Letter to the Front"

CONTENTS

mind

body

mind.

BACK SEAT, 1965   FORWARD, BACK

Performance poem

She looks through the top edge,
the new Ford Galaxy's back window   fixates
on moving light   white balls,
giant pearl onions stuck to wooden posts.
She thinks on the moon's placement
in the black sky, always where her eyes can see,
moon moves with the speed of car,
parallels controlled by destination. *When she's older*
she'll meet "prince charming."
Speeding world outside, she's on
back seat counting. It's safe to count, 1-2-3,
father, son, holy spirit, 1-2-3, father,
son, holy ghost, amen. She makes a tiny
sign of the cross in the air with her six-year-old
right index finger. *She'll walk with*
a limp in nine years.
She always makes a swooping motion, outlining
movements needed to bless the air
inside the car.   Bless the air inside the car
inside the car. Bless
the air
the air   inside the car.   She
reads books   likes to hear words in air. She
blesses the words, counting 1-2-3-
4, needs to even the odds   she counts
to even the odds.   Safe to count an
even number of words that dissipate into
back seat of car, Ford Galaxy,
moon from car moves faster than galaxies,
but she learns the moon is slow   illusion
from back seat. *She'll be a single mother for five years. Eat*
only what her son can't finish.
The American way in a Ford Galaxy
she'll hydroplane at 17.

HOMESICK

She wants
colors: Dunkin Donuts signs
comfort her,
remind her of coffee cups
filled with hot, sweet, milky coffee—

Remind her of home,
          not thinking of fourth grade summer camp,
where she had to recite a prayer three times
or else—
dirty water dripping down
the washroom's roof
          contaminates her.

She thinks of this
staring,
fan grinding,
desk shaking,
in the small, clean room
she rents for the week.

Recite the prayer three times
because once
was never enough—

She sleeps five hours,
not enough time to feel like eating
breakfast with so many strangers.

She remembers reading
interviews of Holocaust survivors
(first-hand accounts).
Captives

drank hot, dirty, diluted brown,
frigid mornings
pressing—
stomachs hardening.

PAINTING CZESLAWA KWOKA

~ In response to Lori Schreiner's paintings of Auschwitz victim Czeslawa Kwoka (photographed by Wilhelm Brasse) and in memory of Czeslawa

In Brasse's black and white photos,
you are a young girl with a round face
dropped into a flat, grey world,
26947 sewn on a striped wardrobe,
naked beneath these numbers.

What does color bring to you?
In color you move through our minds.

In color you are a movie star: Mia Farrow—
slightly protruding upper lip, swollen bottom
forms a dense shadow to your chin.

In color you are a young woman
bleeding from within: pale skin
filters red to pink. This is the
girl you are at Auschwitz, Czeslawa.

You are not a criminal.

~

Your full color portrait
forces our reaction—
your hair is the warmest
fall in a dead winter, amber
background sparks the short, matted
bristles: adolescent questions
quickly extinguished when a scarf adds
texture, diagonal patterns, another
look of a 14-year-old prisoner.

In color you transform: we can

touch your swollen mouth, feel the
voice beneath the left side of your face,
where greys mix with pinks,
a rash of illness.

The contrast holds us.

~

In a soft color profile,
above and slightly right
of 26947, we see a tear
from your right eye spilling down,
just underneath skin transparent,
thin from a bleak setting.

We follow the contour of your
smeared mouth, slightly opened,
trace from lower lip to the
bottom of your chin:
this part of pinkish-grey flesh
appears as number 7.

This is not intentional.

~

In color we feel the
blacks of uniformity,
harsh marks of suffering
blacken the scratched
shadows below your nostrils.

The black slit above your
grey lower lip sucks us
empty—your eyes, black
oval platters reflecting

SS soldiers and worse
within deep, grey carvings.

Black is blacker in color.

~

Painted close-up: a bright
yellow backdrop brightens
the scarf's pattern, your hair
hidden in black and white
becomes strands of sunlight,
movement on still life.

Yellows warm your cheeks,
your forehead clear of dirt,
yellows remove the dark patch
from the tip of your nose we see
in each of Brasse's photographs.
Yellows plunge orange,
settle on the center left of your chest.

You can breathe them in.

THE TOUCH OF THE NOTCH

She'd done absurd things as a child:
the counting of steps up stairways,
the repeating grip of the doorknob in her palm,
always going back to the knob,
going back to the corner of the door,
it had a notch in one of its grooves,
a smooth wooden pool of calm.

She'd rub a circle to the right,
outline the groove,
pray for resolve.

~

When she and her three year old
moved into their first apartment,
she decorated.
Inside the perfectly smooth door,
she gave her son a room
and looked for a hollow
space she could call home.
Ran her fingers down the wood
of every door,
closed eyes searching for indentation:
that invisible worry dump
to help with the nights
of her son's temper tantrums,
the struggle to sleep by herself
before sleep became breaths of insomnia.

No notch in any door.
But she found a green dent
in beige primer on the hallway step.
In odd stillness, her fingers traced
the small spot
smooth like family,
quiet like a gift of understanding.

RATS

Today, sweet butter on graham cracker
reminds me of my grandmother—
Breakstone's in the red round tub,
Italian bread, round loaf from Arthur Avenue,
I drink her sweet coffee,
       eat the coffee-dipped bread,
        feed my yearning for acceptance.
           Sitting at her kitchen table,
              she calls me Lena, Angelina
                  after her.

That's my name up the hallway stairs to her
second-floor apartment, her house on Wilder
Avenue in the Bronx, her kitchen above
the rats in my parents' back bedroom,
my mother has to use the ironing
       board to kill a big one; it comes
       too close. I sleep on my mom and
         dad's bed, afraid to sleep alone,
           afraid Lena of the Hallway will
              take me forever.

Up my grandmother's lime green steps,
I practice saying my real name, "Tessa,
"Mommy calls me Tessa," I whisper,
climbing to the small hallway landing, tiny
corner chair for bad girls who forget their names. I knock
       on my grandmother's tall, white door, feeling
       Lena's dark breath chill my neck. She's shadowless,
         challenges my little-girl rage to help mom kill the
           rats that come at night; she steals the birthmark
              in my brain.

BATTERED

No man who shared his sex with me
        broke me.

Hotel room:
refuge from close quarters

he, pretending to be Scarface,
vigilante, he—
womanizer,
he showed me
on used sheets
washed, dried, stretched, molded into
stark space.

Bathroom   faintly lit.
From behind, he—

rammed it in.
"A wife's punishment," he said.
I looked left.

Wall shadows.
Butter-
colored background
silhouette ass
rod hidden.
Forced flesh until climax.
—*I remember being 26.*

FLAT & HOLLOW

"pain has, or can at least sometimes find, form."
~Maggie Nelson

Pain has form
molds itself
flat on the front
of the daily news
Silly Putty flat
   pink peeling off
   a black & white
duplicate
of violence.
We hold it, stretch it,
the words
killed last night
manipulated by dirty
finger tips,
   those *I*'s strangling us
into skewed horizontal.
Words *woman found*
naked in field adjoining mall
press into pink solidness
flattened by our thumb,
fleshy witness
to what's left out:
below her waist,
   a blackened space
   hollowed out
like eyes sucked dry
by cavernous night,
her edges traced with a blade
to find light.

JOANIE BACH

~ After reading Dorianne Laux's "Fear"

She was afraid of everything: hands—
touch the hands of her old grandmother, flesh
the color of a cloudy sky, her skin turns grey.
Touch the black boy's hand on the kindergarten
line, Catholic school, she turns black. Or brown, his palms
a lighter brownish color, like he dipped them flat
in peroxide every day. Afraid of Liz,
her camp counselor who had no hands,
long arms with long black hair, black as the bottom
of the well behind her aunt's house she squinted
to see, never could see the bottom clearly,

only the black. She was afraid of loving
her camp counselor. Liz comforted her
when she worried about the dirty water
running off the top of latrines;
it would poison her. Counselor rubbed her forehead
with stumps, it was smooth peace like when her
mother held her hand until she fell asleep,
counted imaginary ice cream scoops
to calm her brain. She was afraid to go to sleep
in the black room without the nightlight on. The
closet man held her hands around the bar
in between hanging, Catholic school uniforms.
She dangled in the air, felt the blood rush in between
her thighs, felt like a butterfly scared to fly in the dark.

She was afraid of stepping on sidewalk cracks
or not walking forward the right way. She walked
backward then forward (like she read geese did,
like a caged tiger),
until she thought her mother and father were
safe in the world for another day. They wouldn't
die, flat on the sidewalk, sucked through

the crack, down into hell
because she knew beyond the earth's core was only
the black of concern she squinted to find.
And she knew what that meant but
didn't know how to make her brain
slow,   the sound of a train whistle,
grab onto it and hold. She was afraid

of the horizontal attic door, it left an opening in the air,
she watched the long, black slit grow and shrink
when she squinted her eyes and sat at the bottom
of the stairs. She was afraid of the clicking
in her ears when she swallowed, this was something
no one else heard. Afraid of war movies her father
watched every day, afraid soldiers would lose
their limbs, afraid she would lose her arm
grow another one back, black with brown
palm and grey fingers, she was afraid of
the shadow in the mirror; it fed her replays
of hands she didn't want to touch,
cracks she couldn't avoid,
an incomplete cadence: no resolve.

LADY

My friend's mother gropes a metal grocery cart,
yells at sidewalks, flails her broad arms to the moon.
They tell him she talks to waves—
he waits for the breaking
of her dissonance.

My friend loves a girl but can never
have her home for dinner;
the quiet of family wrestles in his mother's brain—
she rocks at the kitchen table,
legs crossed, right foot numb from blunt stamping
until the noise is all she feels.
She takes to the streets,
salvaging small, coarse garbage,
cart-worthy shards of brown glass.
"The river's skin," she repeats to damp air.

His mother twists her face with the wind,
steps forward and backward five times,
stops to suck the rain:
chin up, lips pucker, eyes close and breathes.
My friend loves rain—
cool layers clean his deep river cuts.
When the bottom drags him in,
the quiet tends.

HOT TEA COOLED

We sat at the kitchen table sipping tea,
me in my twenties
I told my father,
"tea should be hot."
I could never finish it cool or cold.

Hot—
simmered-heat.
I'd gently press
the cup against my face
like a heating pad—
took the pain of TMJ away.

Even as I got older,
in my thirties
years away
from when I showed him books on OCD
when he took an interest in me
because parts of me came from his mold
sharing the disorder
although he never said
never admitted it to me.
We drank hot tea cooled
until my stomach curdled.

But he was my father
he liked this kind of tea,
the kind that started with no trace
of ice,
tea bag boiled,
milk folded
into the beige of the cup's border.
"It's the cold
milk, makes it bad for me,"
I'd always say,

hoping to leave the tea
in the cup half-way
without hearing him grouse,
"God damn it,
what are you wastin' it for."

In my forties
I drink my tea
in dad's memory,
still thinking I should
drink it all, knowing that I won't.
It's my tea, my milk, my water,
my way
to say to him, "I still don't
have to drink it when it's cold.
I'm not afraid to throw the rest away."

WHAT WAS LEFT

My mother watched my father die.
A blender of crushed tomatoes exploded
over the wall, rug, floor,
                              her.

I helped her scrape
red chunks:
blisters off her face.

We pressed towels into the rug,
watched the beige appear
                    like dried sand—
the kind we swept off the docks
at my uncle's marina.

My mother cursed the broken top,
remembered buying the blender for sauce on Sundays.

THE GAME SHOW HOUR

At home, in the quick intervals of my
husband's channel changing,
consonants and vowels toggle
on a flashing billboard like Scrabble
pieces in air. Wheel flaps sound
like those old playing cards
in the spokes of that two-wheeler
I rode when I was eleven.

The *Wheel of Fortune* makes me think
of all the nights my parents dozed on and off,
tired bodies plopped on each other
or at opposite sides of an orange couch.
Jeopardy's final-round theme song
reminds me of the 7-8 pm ritual:
my father stating the questions,
me wanting to change the channel,
my mother, eyes closed, mumbling throughout
the game show hour under her breath.

I watch my husband offer the right guess
to the distinguished host who, no matter
who he is, never seems to age
in the facade of plasma skewing.
Even tired Vanna stays the course:
teeth whiter than any of ours who whiten
every couple of months, blue liners
hollowing out half-an-hour smiles.

And I'm aware of truths: my parents,
dead more than ten years each,
resonate in a glow of TV game shows.
In those interludes of *Jeopardy*,

I lounge, eyes closed, head tucked perfectly
in between my husband's armpit and shoulder.
He helps to ease the ache: solid press of knuckles
against my left breast bone—
my parents' absence.

ODE TO THE MOPEEN

A dampness in the cloth,
a slight weight over
the left shoulder.
It hangs there:
fruited patterns,
colors marred
by coffee stains,
sweat on the edges,
placed strategically,
(the way a daughter
would have learned
to place it),
within easy reach
of another spill.
It stays,
steady on the chest,
until hands grip
the moist fabric,
wipe sugar
off the counter,
guide flour
to the sink,
collect memories
of a mother's routine.

MOTHER'S DAY

Sonnenizio on a Line from Sybil Kollar's "Late Arrivals"

At forty-six I am still the baby of the family.
Still, I wish I could hear my mother say those words,
"You're still my baby." Mausoleums don't have earphones
to hear the stillness that shines on the slabs, the marble walls.
Still, I wish there were some way to know how lovely
and still she lies behind her vertical grave. To ask her,
"Do you still see your features and traits in me?"
I look like her. Still fold the towels in threes—like she did.
But I still don't like to visit her tomb. I'm sure her soul
stands still every Mother's Day when her baby doesn't visit.
As I age, distill like Crème de Menthe left open in a stifling attic,
I can't bring myself to like that ornate stillhouse—its thick air takes my tears.

I never thought I'd want the comfort of a still gravestone embedded in the earth.
I don't. I'd find solace in the sun, the snow's stillicide, my mother's rebirth.

YOUR ATTEMPT

I'm sorry I wasn't there to stop you.

As you try to tell me what you did:
the small toddler chair you've had your seventeen years,
I picture it—a light wood painted baby blue, juice stains on the seat,
fourteen-year-old spaghetti sauce caked on the vertical
wooden spindles that intersect a scuffed horizontal edge,
your fingerprints all over it.

I conjure my own images: the belt you borrowed from your lover's closet—
a short, black leather strap fitting only her tiny waist,
handmade holes added beyond the standard row of openings,
long enough to slip around your neck.
The old, thin metal pipe protruding from the basement ceiling,
inside it, a dark, corroded path for laundry water to expel
into the drywell beneath the house you shared with her.

You call her "The Great Depression." You almost entered
her history, added to a timeline of new male bodies with
withered confidence.

What must have gone through your mind?
Buckle the belt in the farthest hole, *I can't take it anymore.*
Stand one foot on the seat, the other on the chair's top edge, *My mother will cry.*
Deep breath (natural because you thought you'd hold your breath
before your neck snapped), *God, please understand.*
I imagine your thoughts but don't ask to hear them from you.

You tell me your head must have hit the chair.
I envision your right temple accosting those baby blue spindles
on its way to the concrete floor.
Laughing, you say, "I woke up like I was dreaming."
I picture the broken pipe dangling above your nose,
don't ask you for details.

Whenever you recollect that time, my chest caves in,
lungs crushed by all the possibilities,
different outcomes.

I'm sorry I can't listen to the particulars.

HER RITUALS

My ten-year-old daughter's magic number was three; three stood for father,
son, and holy ghost   three stood for safety,
she brushed her teeth morning and evening in threes:
up/down up/down up/down two times,
left/right left/right left/right once (these movements made the sign of the cross).

When she visited her cousin's house for summer vacation
something about being in a strange place
made her depend on 10
morning and evening brush: up/down up/down up/down nine times,
left/right left/right left/right one more   swish water for ten to add to the counting,
her accuracy a metronome, hand movements a soldier eating "square meals."

Morning and evening each day of her visit
she watched herself in the mirror, eyes barely visible
through tortoise-shell glasses splotched with toothpaste.
It was the only way she could make sure the people she loved wouldn't die:
morning brush: count ten   swish ten   spit, *mom and dad are safe at work*
evening brush: count ten   swish ten   spit, *mom and dad are safe in bed.*

After each final count, she spat a foamy, pink mixture in the sink,
watched it fizzle   slowly dissipate,
made the sign of the cross,
and thanked God for everything she had.

CLINIC

I pray for my two sons, *send angels down to guide them.*

awake, 2 am: I worry the high fever
won't go down (my youngest)
worry the girlfriend will make him depressed
    again (my oldest)

unborn I will never know:
when I was 17,
the father asked me to marry him:
older, took me to heaven as I lay under the stars,
made me gasp with pleasure,
more

he was fear, I didn't know it
until the recovery room,
green vinyl recliners,
clinic across from the church
took the fetus, sucked it into silence.

another, I was 27, sibling for my oldest
God forgive me
I couldn't stay with the father,
my mind asleep before they positioned
my legs in cold stirrups
for the dead

I woke, my head bobbing uncontrollably,
Dixie cup of orange juice
gently placed in my hand,
clinic across from the church
took the fetus, sucked it into silence.

a third, when I was 32,
my heart scraped against the father's reaction:

I saw him cry a first time—
he was love, unjudging.

awake, 3 am: I remember when my
youngest was born, saw his father
cry a second time: tears for life,
the undertow of recall,

a cold sweat constricts my silence,
clinic aligned hillside
ceaselessly in my thoughts.

WITH GUILT

she made love to her husband last night   closed her eyes
felt his rhythm fluttering, tongue flickering against
sweet familiar spots to him   unfamiliar to the man
she saw in the dark of her mind

she sighed, mouth opening to the thought of the man's
tapered body inching up her stomach, his dark, soft hairs
dance below his belly button, sweat above her flow
oh   yes   she let him

enter,   a stranger to her body, man with alluring skin,
his arms tell stories in colors: tattoos of skulls, women, and trees,
roots stretching down his long fingers   yes
            do it like a lover

touching lips for the first time   yes   like a swimmer
taking air for the first time   do it,
pressing her mons pubis,   lightly stroking within,
delicately touching the bottom of her sea

she gave it to him like a new wife   anxious, energetic,
insatiable   she gave it to him like an old wife
starved, ashamed of ecstasy in dark places,
carefully handing her thoughts over to no one.

INVENTING DEAD

Small pastel notebook on the bookshelf
words inside blabber incongruence
left behind because I am dead,
lingering at home
like the strong scent of eucalyptus.

Reach for the notebook, want to hoard it,
cannot feel bound pages between translucent
fingers burning.

Attempt to touch the paperclip holder on my desk,
fingers hope to press a paperclip,
be remade as magnet, pull shiny, metal clips
into dull essence, collapsing memory.

Photos of my sons, my husband,
on the wall behind the desk lamp.
I lean forward to kiss
portraits looked at every day,
lips disappear into dissolving face,
a clear shot of Christmas presents
neatly placed beneath the tree,
my family's smiles I breathe into vanishing lungs.

I turn away from these silken memories,
indistinct stomach acid
eats the movement of my thoughts.
Reverse shadows on the linen window shades
dance from the wind outside, spatter white
on the off-white lamp shade.
I understand shadows, appear as shadow,
untouchable.

Dead fades into sound.
Fluid around soul,

a suspended dissonance: mothers' voices,
my voice: air through air through time.
I move through movement, afraid to make
a silent call to God,
waiting for my family to find my substance,
wish it back to middle age,
clinging to soothing discord through antimatter:
the music of Bartok, Varese, Stravinsky.

I turn toward the backyard:
grass as high as the Adirondack chair kitty-cornered near the pines.
Flattened, grassy paths along the perimeter:
household sleepwalks for the dead.
Empty pool unattended, lining faded,
exposed to many summer months of backyard heat.

My husband loved to tend the pool,
dive in cool, clean water, snorkel amid clear chemicals:
his simple mode of prayer.
My children loved to swim,
swift circles, whirlpools, floating on backs,
smiles carried above the water effortlessly.

Absence is hard, comes without granting.
I make my voiceless appeal.

RIVER. SNOW.

~

Yesterday, sound of
toilet flush through the metal
of my window screen,
the late December's snow
assaults trees,
trucks harrow animal death lines
along the road, scattered in 1/2-mile stretches.

"Eva," my mother calls.
"Evanthia!"

"Evanthia!" she shouts,
as I vomit into the undertow of toilet water.

I don't answer, ready to puke again, the river to the east of the window frozen solid;
milky craters transform the water's surface. Hudson River shoreline filled with
military personnel shoveling pink snow into silence. I hear my family's worried
calls, Evanthia?" My young son yells, "Mommy!"

projectile vomit   near miss
my porcelain post

explosion in the river   hit.

~

Two months before we drove to the Pepsi Arena, Albany, NY.   Taconic State
Parkway, curves through valleys. October's passing colors, clear road with deer as
still as air along the road's edges. We slow, in case they dart. Andy, lover, love,
adjusts the radio, broadcasts from the city, warnings I want to ignore. I switch the
station, but Andy's hands grip the steering wheel, pressing it hard. "Eva! We need to
listen to what's going on," he says, readjusting the radio. The drugs inside me fester;
I'm on the other side of Andy's demand, my eyes closed, my mind moving through
the black swirls of the inside of my body. I'm responsible for no one in this
movement.

~

The other morning,
drops of saline down my nose
help the shakes—
bitter, wonderful memory
hits the back of my throat:
the numbing calm of snow
inside   outside—
is the longing for peace the same?

~

Today my mother shouts my name, jarring a new warrior. "Eva," she says. "It's still snowing! A blizzard in the valley! God has said, 'No more…no more war.'" I want to believe her, but my stomach swells as I hear the trucks outside barrel toward the river's edge. I want to believe my body will crystallize, flake into the way it was when I was a little girl.

I stand at the window
fogged over with sweat,
remembering when the soldiers
said I was beautiful
on the outside—
but inside I need
white, flush it through me,
so my war will end.

~

Five days ago, roads were closed to civilians. Television broadcasts warned us to stock up on food, water, batteries, blankets; I'm not sure what else. I learned all this listening to my father and his friend Larry talk as they shoveled. Larry, the neighbor who owns the house next to ours along the river, who told us yesterday that animals were dropping dead along the road. "Something else is going on," he said. "I don't know what, but something's killing them."

Five days ago
I saw Andy for the last time,
I saw the white that brought us together
for the last time,

I watched it snow inside my skin
for the last time.
Five days ago it began to snow hard
along the Hudson River.

~

The army needed to get down the river,
barge cutting ice wasn't enough.
Yesterday the army blew it up,
ripped the river apart,
fish blown from the water,
ice chunks decapitating winter birds
in flight, blood along the shore.

~

Today my son sits on the rug in front of the living room fireplace; he plays war
with his action figures, lines up the "good guys" and the "bad guys." I watch his
quick hands dart through the air, hear his girlish voice attempt to imitate the
soldiers' demands to "Press on!" Today he controls the drama he creates; he is safe
and warm inside my parents' home. Today I am safe and warm in the pain of doing
without, the pleasure of loving my son. I look into my son's stare as his eyes turn
from his toys, fix on a tiny spider   airborne, its transparent web guiding it to lower
ground away from the scorch of the fire. It tackles its own war not knowing the
odds of its outcome.

I understand this,
descend from the flames
in my head, praying
for the snow's fierce accumulation.

Today my mother prays for peace,
my father shovels for peace,
my son creates peace along the hearth of the fireplace.

body

THE NURSE ON PERCY

On the boulevard
moans ricocheted through the first floor
of the small green cottage—
the high school nurse's rental.

Trees with two-toned trunks,
bubbled texture,
seemed to melt as we passed.

Our father told us not to go down that street.
We didn't listen.

My brother and I smoked our cigarettes,
radio blaring from the sunroof of his black Mustang,
Going 40 in a 25.

Our father said if he ever caught us on Percy Boulevard,
he would make sure we never went on it again.
We didn't listen.

He told us not to smoke.
We smoked.
We listened to music he said would make us deaf.
We were deaf.
Driving Percy—
too fast
too loud.
Brassy moans—
music blaring from my bro's car didn't stop the dog's itch
to screw the new bitch across the boulevard.

We felt the hit—
cigarette and spit flew out of my brother's mouth
as he slammed the brakes.

We saw the nurse, "Florence Nightingale" half naked,
run to her beat-up mongrel,
his limbs in curb trash.

We saw our father stop suddenly behind the front door screen
of the nurse's rental.
He shielded his shame, revealed to us the reason why
we always had to detour.

I had an abortion months after giving birth to my first child, his father a man who reminded me of a young Robert Redford—blond hair, sharp yet precisioned nose, blue eyes, rugged gestures of a movie star gangster. He was an unfaithful, abusive excuse for a husband. I hated that scuffed tan paneling in our first apartment, a popular '80s wall covering. It lined every vertical inch. Vertical inches are easy to see with wet eyes. Moisture clarifies vision. I headed down the hallway, that husband caught me off guard, dreaded paneling. Weak knees not because of sex. No sex that day. Because of the ordeal before: strangers, paperwork, waiting room, pamphlets—methods of birth control, diaphragm included. I thought I used my diaphragm correctly. Not mine really, *the* diaphragm—why should I call it mine, possession still nine-tenths of the law? What good did it do? Possess it right, use it right! Can't have other children with scum who spits spat spits at his mother just because. Just because what an asshole he felt like it. But his sperm finagled its way into my body. Quietly, no ecstasy. Quietly, oh God, I tried to make my way into our bedroom, walls screaming for paint, *Cover the fake pine!* I didn't see it—his hand—it slammed my left temple. The paneling opened at each 1/8-inch seam. Took me in. I felt its splinters rip me, right side first. It wanted me as badly as excuses—husband full of excuses, infidelity, hurtfulness. Why do they always want your body? I was a child again, watching Saturday morning cartoon animals take their beatings. I looked for the tiny, white spinning ring of stars that hovered next to illustrated heads. I found the ring. Saw the stars. Realized animators were true visionaries, made my life surreal when needed. Dreaded, fucking paneling. I promised myself I would learn karate, find a new home in the spring.

THE SMELL OF CIGARETTE SMOKE

after sex with her lover
a lingering,
it follows the arc of her arms
stretching across his chest;
they are not smokers

faint aroma touches her thighs,
her legs outstretch
the mattress' steady foundation,
toes molding into beige carpet—
she heads for the bathroom;
she hasn't had a cigarette in years

her lover's cum clots within a short squirt of her pee,
fast flow of what it is they do
each night, a pressing near her nostrils:
tinge of vitamins, sex, urine, then
a break of this intimacy: the smell of cigarette smoke—
she used to hate this smell

in sunlight, sitting at her desk,
she cannot get away from it,
desk edge holds a bouquet of lilacs
her lover cut from the backyard bush,
still, rootless stems suspended in clear water,
brilliant fragrance fed through each tendril
overpowered by the ashy taste that lines
the tip of her nose; she swallows a trace
of another man's smell, invisible

he has followed her home,
a silent dialogue among her senses:
smell, taste, an uneasy passion,
her body begins to like the smell of smoke,
fires grilling her memory until breathless:

the chemistry as he lit up, sucked filter,
blew smoke into her thoughts;
he smokes at least a pack a day

in a soft bedroom light,
her lover and she screw to thunder,
wind blowing the smell of rain
through their pubic hairs entwined—
before the spring storm,
she touches her lover's face,
waits for goodness in his eyes (it's steady),
ashamed of the smoke that finally settles,
stagnant, in this poem.

LADY NEAR THE HUDSON

In the distance
the contour of trees makes
the crevice of a woman's waist,
long, horizontal pose
the undiluted sun tempts.

November, late morning,
oranges, browns more subtle
than the space between her thighs,
a thicket beneath the black of shadows.

In the distance
poised left arm drapes her left ear,
becomes mountain shielding river
to the east.

Large left hip protrudes into sky,
faded reds and russets,
pubic hairs, the yellows of leaves
before falling.

In the distance
the contour of trees molds
a sumptuous lady into landscape,
a fervent terrain,
discrete when the sun shifts.

OCTOBER RAIN POURED ON THE CARRIAGE HOUSE IN GREENE, NEW YORK,

made me want you:
air too wet for horseback riding,
mist catching rides on our clothes.

Taking refuge,
we shared each other
in the warm guest room—
window overlooking the garden,
faded curtains,
Kama Sutra positions
on dated bedspread (used a book we bought at the local bookstore):
private familiarity, but
    needing glasses
to read the captions.

A camel stood in the rain two miles from the carriage house:

In between
llama and horse,
a tanned, muddy hump,
content immigrant.
Visitors welcome—
No one there,
downpours
eating through flesh and bone,
a torrent of grit.
We drove past the camel six times—
none of us
bothered by the rain.

We celebrated another anniversary in Greene, New York:

October, ardent and mature
in the rain, our brief,

shameless collapse.
We agreed next time
to tape Kama Sutra pages
to the ceiling,
(see them more clearly
without glasses).

We rested,
content with the rain's
relentless pulse,
reading at opposite lamps,
you peering through
square frames,
calculating mileage
on the town's map—
me struggling to see
the lines of poetry.

D.J.E.

You turn a corner of my soul,
a weathered page,
although you'd rather finger my body—
smooth   against your hardened male.

Beneath your stone exterior, solid form of the masculine,
you thought to water my plants
when I couldn't—
because of a story in one of my poems.

Our car ride to Maine—
clear raindrops.   Speed against gravity.
You play our wedding songs,
your stern, green eyes perform the romantic.

You turn a corner of my soul,
maneuver my idiosyncrasies like an echo's folded timbre
although you'd rather meander my nipples—
unyielding   along the corners of your mouth.

Beneath my scent, light mix of Ivory soap and rose,
I sail   wanting:
when bodies become words
strong like stone   an undying stimulus.

AFTER SURGERY

Christmas tree lights, a childhood stillness in front of a lit tree
tuck her under a blanket nicely. She's there, resting, waiting for a dream,
   molded into sofa, eyelids burdens to her face.
Purple waves will paint the contour of her left breast,
and places that were once in control succumb
to the tired whole that consumes temporarily.

It's the throbbing of flesh gone.

You're nearby, hot soup on the stove, waiting for love to boil over.
You watch thick bubbles undulate, thinking you'll need to learn
how to touch her more gently. She stares at the Christmas tree
before body trauma hauls her into sleep.

Are you better in the next room during these moments when
the inner stretching points to nothing but numbness wearing off?
Only as she dreams you there, separate from the aftermath.
And she won't realize what an expert you've become
   at folding all the warmth around her.

HEALING

Two weeks after radiation,
you slowly slide your index finger
across your gristly areola,
gently peel the dark brown skin from your left breast.
    Tiny flakes fall to the floor,
an odor, like the smell of dirt in the cracks of a child's neck.

Your right breast: almost ivory, soft pink nipple,
accompanies the ghostly lingering of the left side.
And you're naked in the mirror,
    hairs wet from the morning shower,
armpits damp from sweat already gathering
as you softly rub ointment on your tender scar,
feel the slight indent, gravity filling it in.

You hesitate before getting dressed,
eyes trace the brown scalene triangle
from your left breast, extending slightly
into the shade of health on your right side.
You feel a silence of process: that languid,
invisible sketching of the path
you've taken to heal your body.
It's something like that dream you remember
from childhood: the brook crossing that doesn't end,
    you're caught somewhere midstream,
deaf amid a strong current, cold water
soothing hot toes through sneakers.

THE SMELL OF ALCOHOL

Mount Sinai Hospital—
she watched the stiff tube on the wall
suck memos up over the nurse's station.
Like a clear snake ready to attack,
the tube hung still.

She was afraid,
papers ascended,
end of chute slammed shut.
Suction made her blink her big brown eyes,
her baby fingers gripped my right hand tightly.

~

Before her fevers reached 105,
I saved her from convulsions.
Took her temperature every four hours,
Gave her St. Joseph's aspirin for children,
crushed like orange grizzle in her applesauce.

104 degrees—
her face flushed,
her ear scorched my cheek as I got her ready for the sink.
Tepid water and baby washcloth,
rubbing alcohol in a plastic bowl on the counter,
vapors intoxicated us.

I rubbed alcohol over her tiny body—
stainless shined beneath her little legs,
her hands causing slight, clear waves
to fold against her belly.
I held her soft back,
gently washed her face, behind her ears,
spots burning most,
mixing clear with clear to fight the heat.

Strong, bitter fumes pressed against my temples.
Her eyes stared at something in the corner:
a part of her fever lingering from the day before,
a vision in the air,
the tube at Mount Sinai,
her next trip to the doctor,

where she'll watch the "snake,"
cry, and say, "Mommy, dat?"

~

At the bank drive-thru,
I watch the metal door slide open
like a vertical confessional screen.
Container carries my pay check,
up, down the tube.

She sits in the passenger seat,
a young, beautiful woman.
Not remembering our trips to the hospital,
she watches me watch the check's path.
I see a clear vein carrying her blood
in a fevered body
ready for the sink,
to catch the fever of unknown origin,
eliminate the snake.

I feel her long, strong fingers grip my right hand.
"Relax, we know where it's going," she says.
"Mom, the money'll come back."
I laugh,
check the air for the smell of alcohol.

BENDING

Bottom of basement stairs, open-slatted steps where only deep air understands my questions. She sits on my lap; I'm in jean overalls, yellow sauce-stained shirt, and sneakers. She wants me to be a boy, touch beneath her shirt; I do because she says to. There's no sense in the dark dampness she breathes, kissing me, moving my hand across her young, rubbery back, able to bend into cartwheels, flips, and hand springs. I fade into her damp air, carry her back with me in dreams: I'm always a boy; mud sucks me into roots of trees falling quickly across the backyard. Limbs bending loudly, lonely, no air for safety. I'm always a boy on the stairs in my dreams, her brown hair between my teeth, and she feels it.

CLOSET

Performance poem

VOICE 1	VOICE 2	VOICE 3
Plastic troll house **propped inside,** bellies jut above **a synthetic**	on small, carpeted square dolls with green hair, stubby **diorama**	**two female trolls** big, black bug eyes, plastic legs, **her company.**
A shade of blue **she sees at her back:** mixes	through small, light into black,	vertical gap from her room **dark space.**
She sits beneath dresses swinging back and forth **away from the girl**	worn in May, like laughter, across	Virgin Mary tributes **her place** the street.
She smells must, sisters' Easter bonnets, ▬	Sleeping bag tucked overhead *(she pulls her own hair out ***she hates hats).**	near her two older *sometimes; ▬
Secretly, gently shaking bobbing miniatures, **asking mommy** granddaughter	grabbing both trolls, **right hand** ▬ **what to do** wants to touch	one in each hand **then left,** she practices when the neighbor's her body.

▬ *whole pause*   * *stage whisper*

RIOT IN THE LOCAL HIGH SCHOOL, 1975

Sandra, Martha, & Maryellen.

Sandra turns the hallway's corner, a mass of black
at the other end: teenage girls stampede,

a storm of anger approaching. Sandra makes it
to an open doorway, swiftly slams the burly classroom door.

Her white hands shake against the lock.
She peers through the door's small window,

rage hits Maryellen's white flesh through black turtleneck.
In the hallway   young, black women pull Maryellen's

long hair from roots   fine, light strands stick to black shirt ribbing,
static shock over piping sewn with white thread.

Sandra watches black schoolgirls swarm
Maryellen's thin waist, big boobs, slender legs.

Big, young breasts pound beneath fabric,
Maryellen's hands fight strong fists she cannot block.

Screaming,   her defense falters against bold warriors:
Sandra and Martha's friends who shared a joint the day before,

fire escape behind the cafeteria, discretely pass the small,
white cigarette among quick, waving arms that hurl grey smoke into oblivion.

Martha is black, Sandra's best friend,   like sisters
since first grade. That morning she asks Sandra to stay home.

Martha's voice firm through the telephone receiver, "Sandy, word is
not a good scene at school today; don't go, okay? Or cut out before third period."

Maryellen bobs amid flailing hands, hard elbows.
Sandra reacts like a backdraft, forcing

through door into hallway; Maryellen sees escape
for the first time since she left the girls' room.

Sandra grabs Maryellen's sleeve, hurls her through the doorway,
sleeve catches the turquoise stone of Sandra's bracelet.

In the classroom   door shuts, locks behind both white girls.
Black girls in hallway bounce from door to wall,

knees jam into stomachs, centrifugal force resumes.
Militants on course to the cafeteria. Days before

lunch is served colorblind, Martha shared fries
with Sandra, they lit up together in the third-floor bathroom.

Sandra helps Maryellen up from the classroom floor,
vague ruins of a girl.

They squeeze out the first-floor window,
    softly hit the grass below.

CAITLIN

In memory of Caitlin Boyle, 19, who died November 16, 2005

I see her smile along the river's edge.
In little fragments—like scattered skin.
Not limbs or bones—no dismemberment,
just memories near the mountain's ledge:

its vastness resonating sounds of trains tucked in,
folded with those bandanas she wore to hide her hair.
If you knew her, you'd know the ones I mean.

Her life's remnants line the water's bank:
dance moves because she loved to dance,
her college cheers I'd hear at sports events.
Friends who called her "Caity Bear"
sometimes stagger in the rocks and grooves.

Headphones she always wore hang from a tree.
Near the tracks, her spirit's tantalized, doesn't know
how to reach for them or me.
She's new at death, has much to learn,

before her soul takes its first   eternal turn.

BECAUSE YOU'RE ALIVE

To Valerie, in memory of Tony and Michael

> *Muriel Stonewall 1903 to 1954*
> *She lost both of her babies in the second great war*
> *Now you should never have to watch your only children lowered in the ground*
> *I mean you should never have to bury your own babies.*
> *Dave Matthews, "Gravedigger"*

Your ribs, | split, | as you attempt to breathe,
pieces of your children lost in short lives,
ended because of brutal impact:
    the crash of car against telephone pole,
    Tony thrown from the back seat,
velocity   reaching 90 mph
      thrown into trees, into minutes before his death
        when only one other kid in the car got to yell to him, "Tony, ya alright?"

You would never again see him smirk,
squint his brown eyes before leaving for the mall.

Your blood, ^^jagged,^^ cuts through veins,
through your tough, tanned stomach,
it stretched and contorted to help your babies grow.

Memories   gnaw at your pelvic bone:
    first teeth, first steps,   last profiles within the white silk
of their caskets.

You fight more images of recall: your flight en route to the hospital,
Michael lying in the hospital bed, his commanding officer filling in whatever details
he could, "Broadsided by an 18-wheeler, ma'am. He was *not* driving."
The same side of Michael's face
injured like his older brother who stopped aging at 16.
Your prayer for Mike to see his 21st birthday.

You remember
the stark hospital arrangement,
medical equipment bleeps reality.
Mike unconscious,
   his last movement draws a quick path
from the inner corner of his right eye to his bottom lip.

He dissolves into your finger.

LEGACY

She watered, wiped, clipped,
moved them—hummed old jazz tunes
with her soft vibrato, soothed them.
Gentle green limbs huddled in the dining room
on firm shelves lined with lavender lace,
curtains always drawn for light.
Violets flowered in spring,
spider plants spread.
A small, well kept community until she died.

He walked past them every day.
Silent screams off dining room walls.
Walls she scraped wallpaper off,
picked paint colors (mayonnaise and pink bliss)
to match the curtains.

Her cultivation slowly died:
thick roots exposed, dirt grey,
cracked: a hushed breaking of earth.
White crust covered thin yellow veins.
Burnt leaves fell languidly:
movements too difficult for his untrained eye to see.

VOICES IN DAD'S CHEST

My father sleeps sitting upright on the sofa,
exhausted from working two jobs every day.
I lean on his arm, rest on his worn-out body.
My head gently presses against his chest.
I move up and down with his breaths,
almost doze from his soft monotony.
I'm floating, tiny waves withdraw
from the bright shoreline at Virginia Beach,
currents underneath my ocean lounge.

I hear a whistle in the deep distance.
High pitched, like the gym teacher's blast,
wrong place, wrong time.
I lift my head from my father's bulk,
search for the sound   it's gone.

Again, I soak in his warm, cotton tee shirt,
in the only time he seems docile   compliant,
float off into adolescence until he coughs:
rattles inside his chest, the blow of breath
through thumbs beneath his breast bone.
It draws me to the middle of his torso,
right above his stomach   closer.
I press a little harder, his sleeping body does not oppose.
I tune into his core: gurgling crescendos fade
as he breathes, gurgling fades into voices,
muffled, like secret chatter in the next room.

I close my eyes, listen like a mother to his insides:
mucous in a baby's back my instinct attempts to translate.

But as a young daughter, I surrender to the motes
of sound that help me doze—
that shade his body from the inside,
hide his cancer from the outside.

SHE DIDN'T EAT HER

I

The dog smelled like old socks,
lying on the waxed, wooden floor.

The woman,   dog's best friend,
sat in sunlight reading an old book found in the basement.
She stood to get another cup of coffee,
grabbed her shirt sleeve, ripping it at the seam,
sat back down in sunlight.

The dog moaned, high-pitched
          muffled trill.
Molded into sleep
at the foot of the woman's chair,
curled up, face into her belly like a cat,
for hours.

The woman slowly changed, shifting inside her body,
blood settling beneath skin.
          Something burned in the kitchen:
a shallow singe of coffee grinds had fallen into the pot.

Smelling food, the dog woke, stretched,
her smooth neck undulating, stood on all fours,
yawned a loud, long, shrill moan—
nuzzled against her buddy's arm, nudged
nothing.

The dog remained: nose gently pressed
against best friend's arm until the telephone rang.
The woman would wake to talk, press her lips
against plastic, resonate familiar sounds into the receiver.

The dog moved to the front of the woman's chair,

Her woman remained: long brown hair,
tints of silver along the edges of her forehead
hazel eyes changed into still, black marbles,
whitened folds around lashes.

The dog sniffed,
stole sweet cookies on the side table,
left the woman's chair, headed for the back door,
left a large puddle.

II

Next morning, the dog woke to telephone ringing,
pangs in stomach,
parchedness.
Wedged her light brown nose
under friend's hand,
licked the woman's fingers,
salt,   sugar,   skin.
The dog searched the house,
    no open toilet.

The woman festered
like geraniums,
marigolds,
smelling bitter, fetid.
The dog rested her head on the woman's lap,
sank into thighs.
Bones shifting under the woman's jeans
made the dog pull away,
    feces at the back door.

Telephone rang—

Resting her head on the woman's foot,
the dog gently bruised
toes
in thick air—
a pungent decay
   thick night, hunger.
The dog whimpered as she deeply slept.

III

She dreamed:
filled bowls with food
mouth drool
tasty, chunks for
big brown dog
lapping water
playing
smelling
licking
chewing bones
tasty, sweet
like candy canes
like woman's hands
when she cooks,
Italian breadcrumbs
meatloaf
banana bread
apples
peanut butter,
tasting
woman's toes
after walking in the backyard.

Next day—

"Mom, you there?" the dog heard, slowly staggering to the door,
attempting to bark—
mouth dry as plant dirt on the windowsill.

Her woman's son petted
his mother's dog with one hand,
other hand cupped tightly
on his nose—
gagging
in thick air,   thick sunlight,
smelling mother.

Coffee pot softly cracked above the burner.

ON YOUR BACK

To Toni Turner

Purple wings of a two-inch fly emerge

The harsh pink insect shape   hovering
the muscles to the right of your spine.

Violet diagonal marks below to the left,
as if shadows of insect flight,

Lupus: the bug of your body.

I'm reminded—
Morrison's *Beloved*:

The chokecherry tree on Sethe's back,
"trunk, branches, and even leaves"—
a glaring detail of slavery.

I'm reminded—
perseverance on the skin,
soft lives branded,   involuntary.

HIS PROFILE

Like his father's,   nose less chiseled,
forehead less protruding,   skin
clearing at the end of puberty,
from a distance through a restaurant window
he moves slightly, drops his chin,
his mother's movement,   eyes raise
heavy stare at a parallel emptiness, lips buckle,
press against his jawbone, against
taut nostrils,   flawless regret.

SINGING

I

mother's day, 1995,
troy hit the slate steps,
my husband's back turned
those few seconds when
toddlers walk without
risk

he hit an edge,
jutted blacks, tans
punctured his forehead,
slit a straight line,
opened like a red flexi
wallet (the kind i bought
every class trip in elementary school,
slight pressure of my small fingers
opened and closed its plastic folds)

i looked into troy's
forehead,
wasn't sure where the
inside steps had stopped
before the outside steps began,
my instinct grabbing onto
the moving wall beside me.

II

my best friend helped my husband
find the nearest emergency room,
the wait was short:
an injured toddler, mother pressing washcloth
on opening, takes precedence
over a stubborn grandmother who refuses

to take her medication,
a 14 year old suffering from a migraine,
an old, tattered woman
whom no one else saw but me—
she reached for my hand
as our last name was called,

my husband brought troy
onto the sterile island
surrounded by bright lights,
fabric draped from silver lockets—
i followed, weary of the color white.

III

nurses first,
conversationalists:
"what a handsome little boy," one checked his pupils
"he's so brave," another tugged his ear to take his temperature
"he'll need some stitches; we'll need to restrain him, mom and dad"

a miniature straight jacket (papoose they called it),
sterile white flaps over tiny arms,
little torso, baby legs, pants wet from a soaked diaper,
white wrapped around screams i had never heard before

the doctor on ER duty inserted anesthetic-filled
needle into troy's injured brow before
demonstrating superb sewing skills,
troy's screams—breathless whimpers—
steadied each stitch

the air smelled of hospital:
Lysol, stale breaths beneath a facade of clean,
i sung: "hush little baby,
don't say a word,
momma's   gonna buy you
a mockingbird,

and if that mockingbird
don't sing,
momma's   gonna buy you
a diamond ring"
my voice came from somewhere
invisible.

IV

old woman had followed us,
her hand pressed lightly against mine,
no one saw the dried
paste of her fingertips,
no one felt the smell of her breath
as she hummed,
no one heard her strained voice
mix with my singing—
her rhythm, precise,
carried my voice to stroke the side
of my son's face,
comfort him—
he relaxed for the first time
since papoose swaddled his
gentle body

"and if that diamond ring
turns brass,
momma's   gonna buy you
a looking glass"
troy smiled, hearing the familiar melody,
his cries tapered off
into tones that moved the sterile island
away from the hum of fluorescence,
"momma," he shuddered,
his lips shivering,
eyes beginning to swell,
body limp from drama,
"mommy's here," i answered.

V

across from me
hunched over troy,
the light brown-haired nurse smiled,
her eyes, brown slits of mechanical
pencil lead behind her eyeglasses,
i stood on tippie toes,
giving troy a clear view of my face,
feeling the old woman's stare; she
stood behind the nurse with lead eyes

"and if that looking glass
gets broke,
momma's   gonna buy you
a billy goat"
troy's face calmed, his eyes
moving to the rhythm
of the surgeon and the unseen harmony
shared by woman, nurse, and me

"and if that billy goat
falls down,
you'll still be the sweetest
little baby in town"—
"how wonderful," the nurse whispered,
"i wish you were my mother,"
sweat slowly guided her glasses to the tip of her nose,
her eyes transformed: honest,
large brown pools revealed,
a light swell of tears
settling near the inner corners

i smiled, hummed the same melody,
watched the old woman catch
each breath from the nurse's body,
become the brown in the nurse's hair,
become the voice through the nurse's skin,

humming with me—
troy's body
singing through the white.

NOTES

"Back Seat, 1965   Forward Back" is a performance poem to be read using two voices—readers at opposite points of the room—the second voice, differentiated by italics, to read lines 8-9, 15-16, 31-32, and 34.

The epigraph for "Flat & Hollow" is taken from the acknowledgments page of Maggie Nelson's book *Jane {a murder}*. Nelson thanks "Mary Ann Caws, for her faith so early on that pain has, or can at least sometimes find, form."

"Ode to the Mopeen": a mopeen is an Italian slang word for "a towel usually used to dry the dishes or wipe up a spill in the kitchen" (*urbandictionary.com*).

"Mother's Day: Sonnenizio on a Line from Sybil Kollar's 'Late Arrivals'" was written after reading Kim Addonizio's "Sonnenizio on a Line From Drayton."

"Closet" is a performance poem to be read quickly, staccato (no pauses or rests) three lines simultaneously, downward, three distinct voices for emotional dissonance (the lines will not be coherent to the audience, and this is intentional). Then to be read by Voice 2 from left to right slowly across the page (taking rests when indicated) to tell the story clearly, with Voice 1 and 3 simultaneously only reading what's in bold type. A longer pause should be taken between each stanza. Can also be read silently or out loud consecutively from left to right in one voice.

"Caitlin" is the third sonnet in a three-sonnet sequence entitled "Skin Sonnets." Caitlin Boyle was one of my students at Marist College. *R.I.P.*

Line 10 of "On Your Back" is from Toni Morrison's *Beloved*.

"Singing" contains lyrics from the traditional American lullaby, "Mockingbird."

ABOUT THE AUTHOR

Theresa Senato Edwards lives in Poughkeepsie, New York, with her family. She teaches and tutors at Marist College. Her second book just completed, *Painting Czeslawa Kwoka ~ Honoring Children of the Holocaust*, is a collaboration with Lori Schreiner. Work from this can be found online at *AdmitTwo, Autumn Sky Poetry, elimae, Trickhouse,* and BleakHouse Publishing. The title piece, "Painting Czeslawa Kwoka," won the Tacenda Literary Award for Best Collaboration 2007. Theresa is also founding editor/publisher of *Holly Rose Review* and blogs at TACSE *creations*: www.tacse.blogspot.com.

www.tacse.blogspot.com

ABOUT THE ARTIST

Christine Blu Ashton works in various mediums including oil, acrylic, charcoal, digital paintings and photography. Her work often features the human figure in an attempt to convey strong, sometimes dark and passionate emotions. She is inspired by music and good writers and credits the man in her life (a talented writer in his own right) for encouraging her to continue to create.

www.blu282.com

ABOUT THE PUBLISHER

The mission of Sibling Rivalry Press is to develop, publish, and promote outlaw artistic talent—those projects which inspire people to read, challenge, and ponder the complexities of life in dark rooms, under blankets by cell-phone illumination, in the backseats of cars, and on spring-day park benches next to people reading Plath and Whitman. We welcome manuscripts which push boundaries, sing sweetly, or inspire us to perform karaoke in drag. Not much makes us flinch.

www.siblingrivalrypress.com

www.ingramcontent.com/pod-product-compliance
Lightning Source LLC
LaVergne TN
LVHW091206080426
835509LV00006B/855